Cry Back My Sea

Cry Back My Sea

~~~~~~ 48 POEMS IN 6 WAVES

SARAH ARVIO

ALFRED A. KNOPF   NEW YORK   2021

THIS IS A BORZOI BOOK PUBLISHED
BY ALFRED A. KNOPF

www.aaknopf.com

Knopf, Borzoi Books, and the colophon are registered trademarks
of Penguin Random House LLC.

LIBRARY OF CONGRESS CATALOGING-IN-PUBLICATION DATA
Names: Arvio, Sarah, 1954– author.
Title: Cry back my sea : 48 poems in 6 waves / Sarah Arvio.
Description: First Edition. | New York : Alfred A. Knopf, 2021. |
Identifiers: LCCN 2020048966 (print) | LCCN 2020048967 (ebook) |
ISBN 9780593319505 (hardcover) | ISBN 9780593319512 (ebook)
Subjects: LCGFT: Poetry.
Classification: LCC PS3601.R78 C79 2021 (print) |
LCC PS3601.R78 (ebook) | DDC 811/.6—dc23
LC record available at https://lccn.loc.gov/2020048966
LC ebook record available at https://lccn.loc.gov/2020048967

Jacket photograph by Caracolla / Shutterstock
Jacket design by Janet Hansen

Manufactured in the United States of America
First Edition

In memory of Rachel Wetzsteon

and

for all suffering lovers

CONTENTS

~

Small War *3*

Shrew *5*

Gosling *6*

Animal *8*

Neck *10*

Rat Idyll *12*

Wood *14*

Whorl *15*

~~

Sage *19*

Heart *20*

Nest *21*

Aurora (*or* Ra) *22*

Puck *23*

Bodhisattva *24*

Algarve *26*

Sides (*or* Sidereal) *27*

≈≈≈

Wreck   *31*

Crow   *33*

Peas   *35*

Fey   *37*

Rimbaud (*or* Desert Love)   *39*

Silk Road   *40*

Shah   *42*

Ether   *43*

≈≈≈≈

Kissing Her (*or* Morning Glory)   *47*

Trinkets   *48*

Sinbad (*or* Symbiotic)   *50*

Body   *52*

Hitchcockian   *54*

Aguántate   *55*

Tu Mi Vinci (*or* Hang)   *56*

Sad (*or* de Sade)   *58*

≈≈≈≈≈

Shoe   *63*

Handbag   *65*

Tanager   *66*

Red Dress   *67*

Peacock   *68*

Garden   *70*

Regal   *72*

Nonpareil   *74*

~~~~~~

Sheepfold   *79*

Rodeo of the Rose   *80*

The Rose   *82*

Bed   *83*

Hard Place   *84*

Some Hand   *86*

Go & Go   *88*

Sponge   *89*

Acknowledgments   *91*

Small War

I thought I had left behind the darkness
of the heart   that was a plan   leaving it
behind   I planned to enter the trance of

sensual peace and fulfillment   that was
my plan   But the best-laid plans I say and
pause   thinking it better not to mention

mice   with their trail of dark images   strange
scurry into dark holes   the sense of un-
cleanliness   the gamey smell   a small-game

smell   Oh there's a better word   the game
of the heart   small game   that's good too   like small
arms and light weapons   this is a small war

a small dark and secret war of the heart
Deer running fleet   chased by the hounds
No not that game   Heart war   against all plan

thrusting out of its dark hole   and
scurrying through the room of the life
Scurry or gallop   the sound of horses'

hooves beating on a distant hill   I've heard that
and thought they were running through my heart
Great gallop on the hill   of a dark heart

Though *war* is too great a word   even
"small war"   when we remember the torture
chambers   the real torture   on the real flesh

the bullet piercing the flesh-and-blood heart
There are no words   great or small   to describe
the private torture of the hounded heart

Shrew

I hate my heart   What is this wild and bad
renunciation   I hate my heart   Why
does it hurt me even now after so

much raking over   after so much ruck
It's hard to call my heart *it*   speaking of
part of me that is almost all of me

because what is there that is not my heart
Tucked between my breathing lungs   it beats
it breathes   it is my thoughts   What thought do I

have that isn't folded inside my heart
Is there such a heartless thought   I
don't have one   When I walk I carry what—

my heart on the stick of my body   Or
my courage in the sticking place   Oh screw
don't I have the courage of my good heart

Is this my scarecrow longing for his heart
I'm scared of my heart   the old rags and bones
the rage   a rage for order   pale Ramon

Even though I've raked my heart   it rages
Beshrew me   I know my heart is good   Shrew
little sparrow   will you come to my hand

Oh screw   I eat crow   I crow my heart out
Am I the shrew to it or it to me
To no one but my heart   and it to me

Gosling

I am or I was
a small thing like a sparrow or a toad
or the offspring of something not so small

or the sound of glenn gould humming to himself
these sufferings of a small person wiping her nose
oh soul me

I am only my small humble self
heaving inward and needing to be nursed
a slip of a thing   needing a nurse mother

a gosling needing a mother goose
a ghost mom to come down and be my mom
secretly where no one would gawk with envy

that I was getting more ghost than she was
I was my own goose   not good at soothing
nurses should be soothers   I was not that

having had no lessons not even a hand
or a handout   no helping hand or heart
in the nursery or the gooseries

for hearts' sake and souls' sake   stop sniveling
oh soul me   I am dying to get up and fly
oh sorrow me in a hurry

to the heaven of goslings with their nannies
and sparrow chicks and tadpoles
chicking and poling and sparrowing

a tad too late to play but not too soon

Animal

I am very nervous in myself   I
was always nervous as an animal
angling for its home   and then homing in

toward a home but never finding it   I
was that sort of lost animal   though
animals are rarely lost   We are lost

as they are not   we are the burrowers
in our own dark mud   when yes the light and
so on   Not to be dark or obtuse when

the light is wonderful   This wonder that
we should be so dark and lost   when the world
was designed to be a home for us   Or

were we merely its bad accident   Or
did we come to its great beauty to mar
and obscure   Or did we come randomly

without meaning or message   brought along
by hunger viciousness   And yes the beauty
that we never saw   or that the vicious

never saw   but speaking of myself   I
tried to live in beauty   and found it hard
even harrowing   We are made to drive

at joy and not to strike   and when we strike
we miss   I am nervous as I said   I
wanted all   I struck at it and didn't

hit or battered wildly   and got a hit
Only enough to make me hit again
Lost hunter   sad animal   homing soul

Neck

This isn't done   Grabbing your girlfriend's neck
isn't done   I mean it is done by god
often enough   but not when I'm the girl

or the friend   I love you with all my soul
and all my   I don't know what else to say
my friendliness and my girlishness

but by god my friend   do not grab my neck
Neck with me   nestle your neck into mine
I've been watching the necks of the geese

my geese our geese   flying over our heads
and I've said   goose wander in my chamber
You goose don't be a gander   don't be a

geek   Be a Greek   be a pagan   be
a lover of life   of me   of my neck
Grab my neck my shoulder or my breast

but sweetly if you must   my sweet goose
or I'll call the police   Not that the Greeks
were any better at love than we are

always stabbing at their men and their gods
but my god   better than the Romans
and their strikes at the neck   their split necks

All they did was say do not do   do not
do that   and thwack   off with their heads
So if you ask me what Greek is   I say

give me a Greek over a Roman
oh romance romance   it's Greek to me
it was Greek to the Romans   and to me

to my roaming heart   and my Grecian
gods   to my friends and my gods   and you
you   my silly goose   and my strangler

Rat Idyll

You irascible rascal   O my rat
O rapscallion of my most raving dreams
I had my sights on you   idol of my eye

O rapist of my inner thoughts and hopes
roping me into your kaleidoscope
around and around   around and around

enrapturing my every root and tap
O my satrap you said it   I'm trapped
In my rapt joy   I rally on and on

Sit down I say   but you won't sit down
I sat down and said   sit down and rap
Let me rave you said   let me rave and drink

Let me sleep I said   let me go to sleep
O my scamp I'm sated—what a sad rap
Must never let you get my goat ever

Must be cool when you rave   never get hot
never let you scapegoat me   O satyr
this isn't satire though it almost is

slapstick yes really   a slap and a stick
I know what we need   an artful escape
some far-out art   and some far landscape

not a nightcap or a cup of icy noon
A slow boat to an island or an ice cap
the inscape of an I-land and you-land

Wood

The last thing I ever wanted was to
write about grief   Did you think I
would   your grief this time not mine   Oh good

grief   enough is enough   in my life that is
enough was enough   I had all those
grievances all those griefs   all engraved

into the wood of my soul   But would you
believe it   the wood healed   I grew up and
grew out   And would you believe it   I found

your old woody heart sprouting   I thought
good new growth   Good new luxuriant green
leaves leaves on their woody stalks   And I said

I'll stake my life on this old stick   I'll stick
and we talked into the morning and night
and laughed green leaves   and sometimes a flower

Oh bower of good new love   I would have it
I would bow to the new and the green
and wouldn't you know it   you were a stick

yes I know   a good stick so often   and then
a stick in my ribs   in my heart   Your old
dark wood   your old dark gnarled stalk

sprouting havoc   And now I have grief again
and now I've stood for what I never should
green leaves of morning   dark leaves of night

Whorl

Then I spoke into the whorl of your ear
isn't this love   oh my warlock my lord
Would you call this a war or a quarrel

All those hard words heard in my ears
Our word hoard is harder than a hatchet
heavier than a heart on the warpath

I didn't say you whored me   no not that
I can hear you whooping in the love war
the warping of our words on the field of war

How will you have me   if I will have you
How will you let me   if I will let you
touching my forehead and my temple

fingering my forelock as you touch my skin
I wonder if a whisper is warranted
Will you hear me if I speak in low tones

a hue and cry   will you hear me if I cry
Here here   I mean will you have me here
linking the place with the sound of the word

with the love hoard heard in your ear
This is love isn't it   a war in your ear
love love   a word in the whorl of your ear

Sage

O sage   I know I am   I am a sage
I know unkindness is a selfish act

a straight fish act   or a furtive act
fish or fowl   or a slice of the knife

In the word *selfish* have you seen the fish
I meant to write you a poem of love

green sage gray sage   and sings the silver wind
wing me on the wind   these were all my songs

The geese in their V's are yipping like dogs
along the selvedge of the winter woods

There must be an edge to the self   a hedge
against hell   must be an edge or a verge

Here is the self-edge that you cut against
Here I am savaged   I meant to be saved

O sage   I know I am   I am a sage
I know unkindness is a savage act

Is your heart assuaged   Well mine is not
O sweet   here I am whispering an urge

for the good life   if goodness can be had
the great fields the geese   the edge of the wood

What scraps can I salvage for the soup   When
soup can't assuage there is no love to save

Heart

I lay down and said will you kiss me and
then I cried the tears of the world for you

your heart broken and mine so broken
broken-toy bad and broken-spirit sad

Spirit is a strange word and then the word
broken—for a hard thing—"break a spirit"—

Have you thought what that means—"break a white wisp"—
though I don't know why I say "white" when

it could be any color   *Broken heart*
also defies literal truth   Plump wet thing

and yet it breaks   The truth is what I want
—literal truth refusing metaphor—

to get back to the redness of the heart
though I've never seen a heart in life

I feel it ache   this is a literal ache
Your spirit life   what color has it been

heart's suffering   what color is your stripe
white as a bag or a bone   red as a rag

I wanted to believe and belief too
is hard   Hard enough to break and it does

Nest

And then there came a day that was a day
a world of my wanting with you in it

and all the small creatures came to our side
mewing and cheeping as small creatures do

a day I had wanted for a long time
a small-creature hour in the life of our day

where there were many places to lie down
and sigh and sleep and cogitate and hug

a huge happening among the small lives
a little cuddle with a dream in it

a coddled egg   an apron with a bib
a nest for nourishing the ragged nerves

O robin O rabbit O bat O tiny vole
all flyers and burrowers   come to us now

through our heat ducts and tear ducts and chimneys
come to us with your small-world intentions

that place where only we know how to live
where no one else knows what we say and do

no one knows the crumbs or the flies we eat
or the silly songs we hum as we sleep

Aurora *(or Ra)*

Oh Aurora   Do I live to be adored
or to be abhorred   There's the sun god Ra

who might have adored me   God of the day
Adore adore and the word of gold: *d'or*

I opened a Door and you came in
one morning as a cold sun was rising

O Roarer   I woke to your dawn   my day
El Dorado   my city in the south

Though I love your old gold   I covet
some cold cash to warm me with

How close are the words *warm* and *warn*
And here is a warning   Good morning

O my Aura   Anything may come
O my dawn   Am I a whore to fortune

I whored my joy for the harder days
but what I hoard is never joy enough

I saw the dawn rising   so gold and so red
your golden wallet   and how bright the light

Gold aurora that warmed me in your love
Cold aurora that warned me of your love

Puck

I said to my pontiff on the dark ice
                    wearing on his finger the jewel of ice
                                    as I pondered the smoothness of the ice

I said to my grand high puckety-puck
                    pounding the ice on the dark pond
                                    I said to my pal my pale fire my polestar

you tried to break me so you broke me
                    if you break me again I'll break again
                                    Is there a point you're trying to make

as black as ice on the winter pond
                    I pander to your every pass and wish
                                    You knocked my head off when I tried to speak

then knocked me again for being silent
                    I said to my pal look what you've done
                                    you broke me once and you broke me again

Is there a point you're trying to make
                    as bitter as winter and as ponderous
                                    darling Puck you pushed me far too far

I slid and broke there on the other side
                    on my finger your jewel of white ice
                                  the beauty of the darkness and the ice

Bodhisattva

The new news is I love you my nudist
The new news is I love you my buddhist

my naked body and budding pleasure
in the weather of your presence

Not whether your presence but how
Oh love a new nodule of neurosis

a posy of new roses proposing
a new era for us   *nobis pacem*

O my bodhisattva of new roses
you've saved me from my no-love neurosis

You've saved my old body from the fatwa
Let's lie down in a bed of roses

a pocketful that rings around the rosy
If this is the end of the world my love

let's fall down in bed and die
Let's give a new nod to nothing

Let's give a rosebud to nothing at all
How I love the new roses of nothing

O my bodhisattva of nothing
boding I hope no news but this

For our bodies and souls I hope nothing
but the weather of us in our peace

Algarve

I won't go with Jason for the fleece
for all the algae washing on the beach

gray and silver green and silver gray
all the plastic bottles and old twine

beaching up onto a bed of sand
But there's something rhythmic in the art

an algorithm for an argonaut
an I'll-go rhythm or I'll-go-not

I said I'll go with you anywhere
and I'll come there too if you are there

for where is anywhere if you are there
the washing of the waves along the beach

all the plant life of the ancient sea
the dune flowers silver gray and blue

These are the ornaments of what I mean
the organza of a revelation

the orgasm of a something-rhythm
in the gauzy morning near the sea

Our good bad all garbled algebra
which is the "binding of the broken parts"

which was the offering of Al-Jabr
ergo I'll go elsewhere if you are there

Sides (or *Sidereal*)

You decide please what side you're on
                the sidereal or the earthen side
                          or any other side that sounds like love

or sounds like a sound of turning in bed
                toward your side or my side toward me as
                        I sleep or don't sleep turning toward you

and touching the star side or earth side
                along the slope of your shoulder or hip
                        sidling in and breathing through my nose

turning my face to the side inside your heat
                sleeping like that beside your whole world
                        both sides the inner and the outer side

both sides the stellar and the earthy side
                This is the insidious unreal thing
                        this is the side you really can't decide

the stuff in your starstruck or dirty dream
                speaking from the sidelines during the night
                        talking roughly to me during your dream

Oh dirt dirt Life turn back to my side
                this is real the side of the real our bed
                        please turn toward me real in the night

Wreck

When life is a wreck
with reams of remorse

and thousands of replies
can all the roses and wintergreen and heart

Oh reckless heart
heartwrack

Is it realizable to start again
with our faces wearing their young green hope

A white rose on the bedstand
white curtains ruffling

and the riffling trees
I turn to you and say this: ruffle me

What is this ruffle?   an inner stir
stirring through my life

as if it were
my life

It may be something else
for no one knows

where any stir comes from
or any riff

where any love comes from
or how it comes

Wrecked heart
wracked heart

All the roses and wintergreen and heart

Crow

My only hate   my only love
you like

to chant
chant cant chant cant

Oh my clarion of a summer day
carrion squawk of your old heart

I never cared you carry on
under the blue sky of a summer day

A hell of a day   a sigh for a day
halcyon cyanide day

lying in a field on a summer day
calamitous   calm gaze

Your can't do and nothing else can do
while I cavil   I do   I do

You collapse
in my lap

Oh my lapsed love
you old cuckoo you

Rook me of my heart
oh crooked heart

Oh crackpot heart
oh my clochard my wanton clock

I do not want your do-not-care
I excoriate your do-not-care

I core out your heart
curse you old crow

I know that you care

Peas

I sat in a field full of peas and fed
once long ago

hulling the fresh green peas

and eating them raw
from the palm of my hand

Each a green
                explosion
a kind of green dream

in the peaceful field before my life was lived

fielding the future
              as I grazed the peas

I can hear myself saying
                    please oh please

pleading for something I didn't yet know

Had I known
              I might have said
Give me some fresh green peas

give me a handful of peace

Let me graze
in the grace of the field

Peace peace!
would you hold yours please

Did I say peace and grace

I ask is the peaceable possible

Fey

I'm fey
       no one says this anymore
or this   feckless
               falling into a faint
phantom
            my phantom life
the rag of fantasy
                 the drag
as I feinted
           not meaning to lie
I feel the lure of failure
                the feeling
that all has failed or will fail
           not the allure
maiden fair maiden
             no one says this
when the word
        won't come through
not the word
             or the hope
and no one says why
        fie! No one says this
fo-fum
        or this
            my life is fallow
that feeling
      do you have it sometimes
my life has fallen
               fallow

it doesn't follow
        that the next phase is up
I fell into a foul temper
            no one says this
a sick faint
                sycophantic
the figment not the allure

Rimbaud *(or Desert Love)*

you must walk your thousand miles
Rimbaud walked till his eyes turned white

his mother was a wretch
therefore he walked his thousand miles

boys with wretch mothers must walk their miles
oh love you need your desert eyes

white searing desert eyes
served but not deserved

through the white desert for many days
in a white sandstorm

watching the sand bodies roll and turn
in the white desertifying desert wind

desertification occurs
after the dereliction   after the derision

dear love   your derelict desire
corpus delicti

you must walk your white miles
carrying the body of your offense

Silk Road

May I relax
from the long longing

I have long had
in the seat of myself

now late in my life
in the seat of my love

sagging there
in the soft couch of himself

late late at night
lipping lisped kisses

into his cheeks and his neck
and saying

whatever silliness
sallies from myself

as long as it is soft
and silly and silky

Far down the Silk Road
we have come and gone

across the Bering Strait
and through the unbearable

sailing on the couchboats
with their square sails

on round pegs
across all the continents

of fury and drink
and sickness and dismay

gusting on and on
in the cheeks of our need

with the wind slacking
and our faces slack

sagging there
in the couch of ourselves

a whisker in a kiss
a kisser in a wish

where all that we say
is couched in a whimsy

snapping our fingers
to the sound of a gust

Shah

Pasha pasha you came into my life
and I painted you with my passion

I couldn't make the passion go away
though I wanted to   Oh shah my hummingbird

humming something a human wants to hear
something like those words that have no sound

pushing through the passion with a shout
Push push here you are doing it again

some color in the pit of it
something sham in the pith of it

something like shame in the myth of it
or a puzzle deep in the paint of it

Something pithy and pained in the human bird
as though the words weren't made to say aloud

You paint me with pain   this is what I know
and the shame is where it's pushing from

Pshaw let the bird hum and the hum hum
some human and humiliating thing

Oh passion have patience—do a *pas de chat*—
tell me your story shah   show me your heart

Ether

In the ethereal fields
     the real other realms
          where what is real is air

              where air is what we are

your elbows my elbows
     the four humors
          the four funny bones

              where what we are we are

a rumor of humors
     bodily or bellylaugh
          where we laugh and laugh

              at what we always are

down on all fours
     laughing in our hats
          your more and my more

              all that we were and are

calisthenics of the heart
     athletics of the soul
          aesthete of ether
              either or the other

          of what we were and are

Kissing Her *(or Morning Glory)*

You're angry as a dog
or an angora cat

An anguilla with gills
all eels do have gills

You're angry as an eel
you do not feel your heart

you only pump your gills
I'm surprised that eels bark

sometimes mew like cats
right before the hiss

And hiss rhymes with kiss
short for Kissinger

who was instrumental
in the making of a war

the history and hisses
of a gala glorious war

While you were kissing me
the day was such a glory

Trinkets

First you gave me the jewels
and then you gave me the scars

Why did you want to twist my wrist
right where the bracelet turns

Why did you want to wring my finger
where the ring might have fit

All I have now are the jewels and scars
on the scarp of my life

I'm up or down though I don't know which
I know that I'm injured and scared

I've got them now in a burnished heap
gaudy old glamorous trinkets

with stones and gems from inside the rock
and an old glug of memory to drink

And will there be more glamor
and will there be more drink

in my brace of garments
as I scuff up and downtown

carping and glowing
There's not much to give or say

I'll have some glug and get some sleep
and some life love as deep as a drink

not my life's love but love for my life
I will drink it even if you can't

Sinbad (or Symbiotic)

I'm agog in the synagogue of love
and the sin is I don't know my Sinbad

Is he Gog or Bes or the seven dwarves
He *has* been an assault on my senses

a leap and a slam and a somersault
It was in summer that we fell in love

Love and hate   he can't get them straight
we should be sailing home in a schooner

He needs some synergy between his selves
instead there's ergonomic confusion

He was erotic and he was erratic
he was scintillating and then savage

It's a symbiotic thing   my bio and his
I'll need an antibiotic to fight him

That's a symbol for a powerful drug
No I think I'll need a synecdoche

I'll need a singer in my synagogue
The sin is I've already left the dock

and I think I'll need the seven voyages
Szymborska could write this better than me

I'm banging on my cymbals and crying out
Saudade saudade is what's coming for me

I have to go now—though how I don't know

Body

part bone &
    part bomb
yours is all sore
    & ready

not a tin can
    or a cocktail
yours is atomic

a bomb
  made of your atoms

I have a diamond
  you have an atomizer

of the anatomical
   & soul
     being

concording your soul
     atoms

into a sole
   bomb
  for atomizing my soul

with its adamant
    gleam

I'm toeing around
    & avoiding the pulse

so as not to jig
        the trigger
or tip the jigger

this is a soul bomb
      solely for me

arraigning my brilliance

why do bombers
      bomb
      a beauty body

Hitchcockian

stop staring stop staring
wagging your head and talking lies
why don't you do some staring at the stars
even your cock is a crowing liar
trying trying to hide your cry
the cry of a bad hatching
that hatched you
as you are
not as you should be
can't you fall down the hatch of your heart
into the hole of the hell of it
can't you hitch your cock to some high pole
a maypole for maying
not dismaying
can't you hate your hatcher and not me
a hatcher is a mother
yours was a hatcheck girl she had all your hats
and would not give them back
oh somber sombrero
and your heart is the worse for it
even your soul is hitchcockian
though he had a bowler
you have a howler
give yourself a little heaven
as you should be
not as you are
go hitch a ride on a star

Aguántate

Did I want a glove   or was it love

a globe of love a lobe   no not a glove

I wanted a globe a world   I got a glove

Take off the glove   Try on some love

This is global and local   This is my life

I want your bare hands   on my lobes

instead you're lobbing me   a lot of hell

So you like making love   with gloves on

How bad it feels   as hard as hooves

I'll give you the beef   I'm all beat up

Too much to bear   my gloved boy

Here's the skinny   I want some skin

but love me   with your both hands bare

Oh beglovèd boy   turn a cheek

Tu Mi Vinci (or *Hang*)

You hang me on the hanger
of your anger

like da Vinci's triangle
and *vinci* is vanquish

and vanquish is
like anguish

and hang
is what we do
to criminals and clothes

Is it a crime
to hang round your neck

staring in your eyes
and kissing your lips

Here I am hanging
naked and splayed

I'm hung up on you
you're hanging me up

There's no other angle
I've flung them all out

You've taken my self
and you've hung it

in the triangle of you
where I'm dangling

I'll go away
in a new set of clothes

for a cocktail or a crime
does it matter

but please let me down
off your hanger

Oh love let me be free
of your anger

I'll hang a round sign
Now I Am Mine

old words
you can't get the hang of

Sad (or de Sade)

So it's over now   that's what you say

How sad to say   what isn't so at all

nor should it be   I'm saying this to you

I'm saying I love you   and you love me

It's sheer sadism   to say this isn't true

which is what you say   at least once a week

wanting to persuade me   to be sad like you

My desideratum   my sole desire

O saturnalia   of sad desire

I love you satanic   and sweet as you are

siring and stirring   my distraught desire

I'm your Sadie   your sweetheart   your girl

How could I hate you   because you're sad

Sad to say   to say and do   I'm sorry

you're sad and sadistic   you're sorry too

Or I think you're sorry   that's my sole hope

Monsieur de Sade was sad   we all know this

That's how he got   his satisfying name

And aren't we all   am I not   aren't you

wanting to live   a sane and hopeful life

Oh my Sade   How sad   you are   sad I am

Truly sad to see   you are as you are

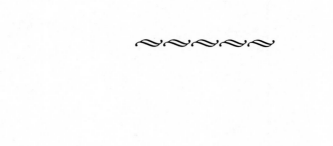

Shoe

I was going to meet my own death
and it stood me up

Or that is I stood up and said *not now*
Some days I know I won't stand for it

Can you stand the thought of being dead
some days I think I'll take it lying down

Sometimes it's good to take a stand
though I think I want a standard-issue death

Shoe in   shoe out without a horn
or play me a horn as I go and come

Or maybe not you but someone else
whose job it is to usher me forth

Stand down I don't know what this means
Stand up and soft-shoe across the room

The issue is   well do you like your life
Oh hand me a tissue I do want to cry

There's no such thing as a stand-alone shoe
There are always two to cover feet

Think of not knowing how to feel
think of that while dancing on your heel

Death might not be up or even down
it could slip in sideways   it could shuffle

It could stand very still
like a life on the stand of the world

Do hand me a tissue or a handkerchief
I don't know whether to wave or cry

I don't know whether to live or die
it could slide sideways after all

Like two shoes dancing in the living room
or two heels hopping in the dying room

Handbag

I felt some desire and I lost my cents
it was expensive to feel so much

I lost my sense and my money   I did
not consent though it was consensual

It was a con and it cost me my self
I was selfless I was trailing a scent

I was moaning but not for the money
and that's a mistake I lost my sole take

and now there's nowhere to stake a claim
I'd put a stake in his heart but I can't

O Bacchus will you dress me in grape leaves
I'm back to the bar to begin again

and needing a quaff of some rich stuff
and some hair dye and a bewitching scent

and all that is sensual and cunning
without a cent or sense in the world

and nothing in my handbag but my soul

Tanager

This was the year I saw the tanager
flitting out from behind a tall tree
like Tanny Le Clercq wearing scarlet
and then turning she twirled and was gone
cutting a tangent through the sky of my life
and the effect was as tangible
as a trip to Tangier
This was the year
of bright change
the year of the dress
the lovely fire-red dress
and black shawl
that would take me
to the sunset or sunrise
And it moved in me
like Tanny Le Clercq
fire tones leaping
in a fiery thrill
Wouldn't you live
for a tangential thrill
that goes to the skin
and bones and sex
to all the bright points and
colors of your life
I had seen it in books
—the tanager—
a bright black-winged cry
bringing me up
to its tablet of joy
its template of joy
its plateful of fruit
The tangerine tanager
that should be its name
and how do I eat it and dance it and do it again
this once-only moment of life

Red Dress

It's wrong to live wrong   I was thinking this
and wringing my hands   I wrung my hands

Wasn't it right to live right   and to write
about the right life   rather than living wrong

and writing about the wrong life   Which is
righter which is wronger   The thing is

if you have the wrong life you don't want
to tell   thinking always that somehow you

will right it   Righting and writing it's a kind
of redress   a new dress I'll put on when I

rewrite my life   I'll run out and get it now
while there's still time   a red dress for joy

a red dress for redress   and I'll dress you
down as I walk out the door   You'll ring

and ring but I won't rush back   I won't
write back   You'll be right and I'll be

wronged   and that's what I'll tell if I get
the time   but not to you   you won't be told

You can read my redress in the papers
I'll be out on the town in my red dress

Peacock

It sounds like a part of the body
doing something that it has to do

not like a vegetable or rooster
more like the male part of the male body

riffling its wheel   flaunting its eyes
every feather the figure of an eye

many   like the arms of a Vishnu
many   like the breasts of Artemis

O heaven and all the lotuses
the hues of all-prismed reflection

with a keen that pierces the garden
And this is the bird with the name

that's also the name of a penis
that is peeing   the peacock peeing

Why don't you meet me in paradise
the place of the parrots and dice

the place where we go to die and sing
the place where we go to sing and die

Apparently it's all pure there   all joy
pure as my heart when I look at you

right here in the throne of the pleasures
The peacock tilts its fathomless eyes

and then folds its great fan and departs

Garden

You could say a garden is a garden
but guard against the place where anything

is what it is and nothing more   A garden
can be avant-garde or not avant at all

or from a vantage that never mattered
except to the gardener and no one else

It could be a place where Adam and Eve
were happy though not yet fulfilled

Nor would they ever be if history tells
us anything at all   If the bible can be

called history   Let's say it can because
it belongs to the history of our souls

And so there they stand naked and the snake
and the penis are one and the same

It can snake through your garden and take you
places where the flowers sometimes go

to that bliss of fragrance and bee-buzzing
or else can be a hisser or a hater

or a pisser and really mess things up
and mow over your pretty violets

And while you are there guarding against
the gorgeous or the garish or whatever

something insidious is going on
and insinuating and undulant

Much as you may love and guard your garden
there is no protection from its power

En garde! Kiss the gardenias and hope

Regal

There are some violets in the grass
    purple and pretty and in the grass

and now I notice that the violets
    are the color of a bruise

They are pretty but not quite a pensée
    and violet we know is not quite purple

They are a posy of my violation
    or the bruise is the color of violets

and you are posing as the lover boy
    who brings the posy of all pure joy

This is a position a person can take
    almost as joyful as anything

and voilà   this is my enviable life
    the veil of my lovely and loyal life

This is the question I'm trying to pose
    about life behind a veil of invective

I don't want to say a vale of tears
    or a walk through the valley of death

Shouldn't my life be inviolate
    not kicked and insulted and royal

the purple regal of the royal house
    Aren't all our lives made to be holy

and royal almost always is violent
    The queen of the grass is deposed

Nonpareil

for Linda Ollerenshaw

How I wish I could be something else
I seemed to change I had to have changed

and yet *plus ça change plus c'est pareil*
I wanted a cup of dark tea and a nonpareil

I wanted a life without a parallel
a peerless and unparalleled life

made only of chocolate and sugar
on a dark night pearled with stars

and I got it just like everyone else
as though getting what was coming to you

could really be what anyone gets
I was on the parallel bars turning

over my own self and then turning back
but that was many years before I changed

into the one I am now who's turning back
through her own life to find the nonpareil

as the past smokes up from the dark tea
Did I get it just like everyone else

with a sip of dark tea and a nonpareil
Am I both the same and something else

or had I gotten it like no one else
exactly what was coming and nothing else

Sheepfold

It's so cold here   and there's the snow
he doesn't like snow   he's from the tropics
there's ice to be precise   there are icicles
he wants it hot   he wants the tropics
he keeps saying it   over and over
she is thinking that this is a trope
or *de trop de trop*
she does know   she doesn't know
he does know   he doesn't know
say this all fast   and it will be as snow
as white and cold and as ephemeral
all of their truths   will be as snow
the trees are black   in the winter woods
and now they are passing the sheepfold
white sheep and black sheep mingle together
they are a tropism   all turning one way
and fold is a word that she desires
fold and wool are things that she desires
but there is much cry and little wool
the sheep are running as a herd
their little hooves pounding the white snow
she needs to be careful she thinks or she'll die
of exposure   out here in the cold
the ram is out ahead   there's only one of him
but here they are now   the two of them
you snowed me she said   which meant he had lied

Rodeo of the Rose

It's like I fell off the horse of my life
I was horsing around and he bucked me

I went over sideways or backwards or
I don't even know how I went but I

went   It's like you don't know your own horse
It's like you're riding along and he rides you

He keeps at it and at it till you buckle
and break a rib or a toe or a heartbeat

Never mind that I wanted to be soothed
and suckled   never mind that I wanted

to ride and ride replete with life joy   Ah
ah Ay ay all the sighs and gaspy breaths

when you're riding full out on the joy path
But there are folks who can't bear the joy

the rippling riveting enchanting joy
They've got to buck you till they flip you

They deride you and they deride themselves
Whose horse was this anyway   Wasn't it

mine   Or was there someone else somewhere
leading them in and handing them out

glad-handing the folks at the rodeo
A grand master of disaster and desire

carrying a whip and a full-blown rose

The Rose

You took me
in the bloom of my life
& unbloomed me

not the unbloom
of deflower

or the
denude of undress

I was dropping
my petals
& saying
yes yes

There are only
so many petals
they won't last & last

& the hub of the flower
is as bald as a bone

& now I am
the node of disarray

the nub of despair

I was love & beauty
I was plucked in a pose

I was taken from a posy
I was not loved   I was loathed

Bed

I haven't got a fingernail or bed
or even the bed of a fingernail

and I was hoping that you were the nail
that would hang me up on the joy wall

and I was hoping you were the finger
that would point me toward the rainbow

as the rain bowed and slashed and all
the colors stood still in the singing wind

I haven't got a mailbox or a box
for my files or my fingernail filings

I haven't got a box of photographs
or a graph of the days of rage and pain

or only on my heart which hurts me
I haven't got a file to cut off the chain

or a ring   I wanted a ring and a song
a bed with a head a heart and a soul

though there are so many places to sleep
I have to say you hit the nail on the head

and that was my nail and my head and now
I am dead   there are so many places to sleep

I have fallen from the joy wall and died

Hard Place

I won't leap off the edge though people do
and how sad it is for all of us

that they didn't know how to live
when life was so full of all of life

which is what life is full of always
for when it is full of something else

something like ugliness or lies
then it's also life but not life

and this is a distinction hard to make
like a rock and a hard place

and the rock would be for leaping from
and the hard place for staying in

if staying can be said of hardness
or leaping can be said of rocks

and all I wanted was to be rocked
to be soothed and rocked in a hard place

and it isn't the hardness that does it
there is nothing that is hard in soothing

it should be easy but is hard to find
it should be soft   soothing should be soft

even in a hard place   this is the truth
there is no place as hard as a rock

and nothing as soothing as rocking
and this is one of the paradoxes

that come to the hardest of lives
from the softest of thoughts

there's no place so hard as a hard place

Some Hand

I saw him go out handsome in his suit
                              in his shoes and suit so handsome

he was hiding something in his hand
                              when he turned and went and he said

I'm going now   I said will you give me
                              a hand and he was walking out in his shoes

and his summer suit into the spring day
                              and I thought he feels better today he's

wearing his lovely linen summer suit
                              it suits him and so do his shoes and then

I went upstairs and I saw in his room
                              that the suitcases were gone and so were

his hands and some of his clothes and
                              some of his shoes and some of I didn't

know what   It's shoe in and shoe out
                              handsome devil with something in his hand

and it's the soft touch of the nest of
                              his hand or it's the tough stuff in the stuff

of his hand and I said will you give me your
                              shoe and he said sure and hit me on the head

with the shoe and sure it didn't hurt it was
                    barely a slipper this was a slip-on and slip-off

this was the soft sole of the dapper world
                    Tap-tap dap-dap or dip down I kept saying

why don't you dip down into your deep self
                    and tell me why you're so handsome and why

so devilishly angry there's a story there
                    but it doesn't suit you to say what it was

and now you've got your hand on the knob
                    in your dapper suit off into the spring day

Go & Go

one person in the universe

        can be the universe

one turn or one verse

        like turning over in bed

or turning in a dance

        the unique & united

one niche of your life

        the one single hub

of your universe

        the unicycle that wants

another wheel

        or the cyclonic

disruption of all the lines

        the body flying off the cycle

& rolling on the road

        oh pour me some please

a big unison drink

        a big gulp for two of us

staring in one glass

        as the cycle turns

& each turn says

        life love life love life love

a niche or a nest

        in one old bed or old tree

all the arms going up

        & stretching in sleep

& all going around

        like branches in a wind

all go up in the end

        all go down

they go down in the end

        they go & go in the end

Sponge

Soul like a dirty sponge that soaked up all the dark bits
from yours   all messed up and mixed in

with the dirt of the days   the old hairs and hatefulness
Oh my god I knew there was hate in the human world

but I didn't know it was the job of my soul
to clean it up   How can I clean it up if my soul

is the sponge sponging it up   In the end   it doesn't
go anywhere except into my dirtier and dirtier soul

And I say   well   crying will clean it up   but then I'm
bent over crying because my beautiful sponge of a soul

that lay in the depths of a cool warm aquablue tropical
sea with little fishes flitting about in their exquisite

jewel colors   and rays of sunshine raying through
has been used to sop up an angry man's leftover

cruelty   Yes   cruel does sound like jewel and there
should be a jewelry   How can I squeeze it out   I'll

need a new sponge   but I can't throw out my soul and if
each tear is one drop of an aquablue tropical sea

maybe I can cry back my sea   It's not so easy
to clean a soul   some say weeks   and some say centuries

ACKNOWLEDGMENTS

Love and thanks to the late Mark Strand, the late C. K. Williams, Edward Hirsch, Page Starzinger, Rachel Eliza Griffiths, Dennis Nurkse, John Koethe, Alice Quinn, and above all others, my editor, Deborah Garrison.

Thanks to Victoria Pearson and Todd Portnowitz.

Appreciations to Janet Hansen and Pei Loi Koay.

Special thanks to Roy Skodnick and Frank Gillette.

I would also like to honor here the late Ralph Angel and the late Leslie Wolf, my first poetry teachers.

Thanks to Jesse Littlejohn.

~~~

Special thanks to the editors who published these poems, some in earlier versions:

"Algarve" in *TriQuarterly*, final print issue

"Animal," "Gosling," "Rat Idyll," "Shrew," and "Small War" in the *Boston Review,* winners of the 2008 *Boston Review* annual poetry contest; "Small War" and "Animal" also on *Poetry Daily* (poems.com); and "Animal" on howapoemhappens.blogspot.com

"Bed" on *Plume* (plumepoetry.com)

"Bodhisattva" on Academy of American Poets' *Poem-a-Day* (poets.org) and in *The Best American Poetry 2015*

"Handbag," "Neck," and "Wood" in *The New Yorker;* "Wood" in *The Broadview Introduction to Literature* and in its *Concise* and *Poetry* editions

"Sage" and "Whorl" in *The New Republic;* "Sage" also on bestamericanpoetry.com; "Whorl" in *Laberinto,* the *Milenio* cultural supplement, translated into Spanish by Víctor Manuel Mendiola as "Espiral"

"Red Dress" in *The New York Review of Books*

"Wreck" in Knopf's *Poem-a-Day*

Sarah Arvio, the author of *night thoughts: 70 dream poems & notes from an analysis, Sono: Cantos,* and *Visits from the Seventh,* and the translator of Federico García Lorca (*Poet in Spain*), is a recipient of the Rome Prize and Bogliasco, Guggenheim, and NEA fellowships, among other honors. For many years a translator for the United Nations in New York and Switzerland, she has also taught at Princeton and Columbia. She lives in New York City.

A NOTE ON THE TYPE

This book was set in a typeface named Bulmer. This distinguished letter is a replica of a type long famous in the history of English printing that was designed and cut by William Martin in about 1790 for William Bulmer of the Shakespeare Press. In design, it is all but a modern face, with vertical stress, sharp differentiation between the thick and thin strokes, and nearly flat serifs. The decorative italic shows the influence of Baskerville, as Martin was a pupil of John Baskerville's.

Composed by North Market Street Graphics
Lancaster, Pennsylvania

Printed and bound by Lakeside Book Company
Harrisonburg, Virginia

Designed by Pei Loi Koay